A to Z
Of
BDSM

A Practical Guide to the Art of BDSM Play

A to Z
Of
BDSM

Bill Reed

To Anita, my love and my life, for life.

And

To the most wonderful Leather Family a person could belong to.

Also

To the Members of Tulsa Dungeon Society, a BDSM/Leather education and support group.

A special thanks to the Cover Model and Designer, my favorite "cane girl"

And

to the Photographer, "Tater Salad"

Preface

I would like to begin by giving you an idea of what I intend with this book and how it came about.

I started writing articles for alt.com and bondage.com. You might say that this is a compendium of those articles as well as some added materials and thoughts. The articles were very well received on both sites but I felt that the articles were reaching a limited audience and I wanted to reach out to more of the community.

The articles are somewhat of a how-to for various BDSM types of play as well as my own thoughts on a variety of topics. I hope that with these writings I will help someone along the way.

I would like to say that when playing or doing a scene that is described in this book, you do so at your own risk. I assume no responsibility for any injury or damages that you may suffer or cause through your own negligence or lack of skill. I fully recommend you partner up with someone who has been in the lifestyle for some time and is knowledgeable in the practical aspects of play. Mentorship is a great tool and I fully support it.

The following chapters are a mix of beginner to expert and some edgy type play and topics. Enjoy this book and great luck on your journey.

So you have met the perfect one online, now what?

Safety when meeting face to face.

"S/W/M Dashing, Debonair, Made of money. Charming, Witty, a Greek God Physique. I have Skills that would make the Kama Sutra look like amateur night. Can tie you up, wield three floggers, pull your hair, and make you have multiple orgasms with the snap of my fingers. I possess the magnetism and powers that make you want to serve me without question and with the desire that is deep within you. "

Sound too good to be true? It really is too good to be true. When writing a profile, I can be anything or anyone I want to be. I can look like anyone I wish to, even to the point of using pictures that are not of me. I can be male, female, hung like a stallion, trained by top secret BDSM monks from a Tibetan English Japanese House, or any other thing my heart desires. How to you separate fact from fiction? How do you stay safe? I hope to give you some tools to make this a little bit easier.

You have read the perfect profile. The person of your dreams finally is within reach. You begin chatting. Where do you go from here? There are things you should know before you give out too much information. There are precautions to take at that first meeting and beyond. I would like to address all of these things because I feel that safety is paramount to any good relationship, especially those that form online.

To begin with, ask questions. When you ask the questions, listen to the answers. Do they add up?

- "How long have you been in the scene?"

If a person tells you they have been doing this for 20 years, then they should have plenty of references from others in the lifestyle and should be willing to provide them.

- "How experienced are you?"

If they tell you that they have years of experience, then they should be quite knowledgeable about the scene, both with terminology and technique awareness.

- "What is it about BDSM or the scene that you enjoy most? The exchange of power? Role playing? Kinky Sex?

If a person is not entirely new to the scene, they should have a good idea of what it is that they enjoy about the lifestyle. There are many facets of the lifestyle and most of us have many interests, however, we do know what we like and are willing to share that knowledge.

- "Who/what are you looking for?"

I should have a good idea of whom or what I am looking for. If I want a submissive, slave, pony girl, service person, or whatever suits my needs.

When you are talking to the other persons in chat or IM, look for clues that should send up Red Flags when they occur:

Is the person you are talking to rude and domineering?

Does he/she seem to be avoiding questions or hiding things?

Do they seem to change stories or contradict themselves?

Are they ready to begin the relationship from the first meeting?

Does he/she laugh off your safety measures and concerns?

Does he worry about being seen in public with you?

Does he make excuses regarding participating in local group munches or other events with other lifestylers?

The list is endless when it comes to things that should be red flags regarding meeting someone. One of the biggest tools that you can use is your gut feeling. If it feels too good to be true, then it usually is. If it just seems like something is wrong or being hidden, then it you should look at those feelings and not dismiss them too quickly.

When it finally is time to actually meet someone in person, there are things that are quite necessary in order to do what you can to keep yourself safe. Location and Safe Calls are two examples.

Always meet in a public place. Make sure that it is a place that is well lit and crowded like the mall, a busy restaurant, or something along these lines.

Bring a cell phone with you.

Don't leave your keys, wallet, or anything with personal information unattended.

Don't leave with the person to play, go to their place for a drink, or any other places that will put the two of you alone.

Make sure you are not being followed when you leave the meeting place.

Have a SAFECALL in place and make sure that you respond.

Safe calls are of the utmost importance. A good guideline is as follows:

First, if the person you are meeting objects to the safe calls or laughs them off, end the meeting or cancel it. If your safety is not important to the other person, then that person does not have your best interests at heart and that is a big warning sign.

Make sure that the person that is your safe call contact knows your information including your car information and tag number.

Make sure that they have all of the information on the person you are meeting such as:

Name (real and screen names)

Address and phone number

Age and description

Where you are meeting

When you are meeting

Make sure that you have agreed on code words to be used in the safe call. One should indicate things are ok and one for needing help. Those code words should be words or lines that will not give suspicion if they are used.

Safe calls should be made several times. Within 20 minutes of arrival, 30 minutes after the first call, and again after 30 more minutes. You should also make use of safe calls when leaving and then again after clear of the place and once sure that your not followed.

Make sure that you know your safe call contact quite well and that they are dependable and willing to follow through with the calls and notifying the police if something is amiss. Remember that safe calls are not going to guarantee safety but they are a great tool combined with common sense and good judgment.

Please keep in mind that there are a lot of sincere people in the lifestyle that want to meet others. There are also predators, users, and abusers out there as well. If we are careful and diligent in our choices, we have a much better chance of meeting the right person(s) to fit our needs and desires.

You've made it To the Party, Now What? Scene Etiquette

Floggers striking skin, whips cracking and leaving their marks, naked bodies bound in various positions. The scene is surreal, the music mysterious, the sounds of passion a song to your ear. You're new, you're nervous, you don't know what to expect or what is expected. Your first time at a play party will be possibly the most memorable. These tips will help you to make it your first and subsequent visits most enjoyable.

There are some things that are very important to remember when attending a play party, whether at a dungeon or in someone's home. Remember that each dungeon or host will have their own set of rules to abide by. If you are not sure, ask. It is far better to err on the side of caution. Following are some basic tips to make the dungeon experience better for everyone attending.

1. When arriving for a play party, please use discretion in your manner of dress. Don't show up with just a leather harness and all of your business hanging out. Most places that are hosting play parties have neighbors that might not appreciate

seeing your "business." Once inside, the mode of dress is up to the hosts. There should always be someplace to change into your fetish attire.

2. Also try to transport your toys discreetly. I have used suitcases and hard shell gun cases for toy storage and transport. Duffel bags and sports bags work well also.

3. Do not touch things that do not belong to you without permission. This includes toys and submissives. Just because a person is a submissive or slave, that does not mean that they are your submissive or slave. You still have a duty to treat others the same as you would in the supermarket, library, or anywhere else. If you don't know them, you don't touch them without permission. The dungeon is no different.

4. It is not acceptable to touch the collar of another person's submissive or slave. In a lot of communities, this is looked upon quite negatively. If you are unsure, feel free to ask. It will go a lot further in the long run then just assuming or taking it upon yourself.

5. Remember that the dungeon experience is a special time of bonding for those in a scene. Keep talking to a minimum in the dungeon area. Do not interrupt or attempt to join a scene in progress unless you have been asked by the Top to do so. Don't walk up to a scene and attempt conversation with those in a scene. Remember that scenes are not done when the implements are put down or the bottom is untied. There is a period of aftercare that is needed. Give the couple time to unwind, cuddle, and come back down to earth before approaching with any questions you might have.

6. When you are playing, don't hog the play area. There might be other people waiting to use that cross, sling, bench, or other piece of furniture. A lot of times there are more people that are wanting to play then there are play spaces. If you use one piece of equipment all night, you cheat someone else out of there experience. Be conscious of others.

7. Clean up after yourself. If you use a piece of furniture and you are doing something messy such as fisting, wax play, blood play, or something of that nature, be sure to use a drop cloth or towels and clean the equipment afterwards. Remember that people sweat, come, get wet, etc. You need to be aware of bodily fluids and be willing to clean them up. Cleaning items such as alcohol and paper towels are usually available. Clorox wipes work quite well for this.

8. Don't leave your toys lying around where people might trip on them or step on them and break them. Make sure that you move them out of the way before the next scene begins.

9. Remember that we all have lives outside of the dungeon. Leave whom you see and what you see in the dungeon. There is nothing that will make you unwelcome faster than breaking party confidentiality.

10. Offer to help set up for future parties. It is not easy to host a party, especially when you have equipment to set up and furniture to move. Most of the time your help will not only be much appreciated, but it will get you invited to future parties. Helping to set up or clean up for a party is not a submissive-only thing. Don't be afraid to get your hands dirty just because

you are wearing the "Master" or "Dominant" hat. Your help goes a long way as well.

11. Most parties have a DM or Dungeon Monitor. That duty is assigned to someone that has experience and has been around a while. Their job is to insure the safety of all involved and to make sure that the rules are adhered to. If the DM gives you instructions, please heed them. If you question what he or she says, pull them aside and do so in a discreet fashion.

If you follow these guidelines and make yourself aware of the play party rules, you will find that your dungeon or party experience will be quite rewarding and you will enjoy some wonderful friendships with some great people. I have attended a lot of parties over the years and attend the local group's parties monthly. The guidelines that I have mentioned above are quite common all across the country. Be yourself, play safe, and most importantly......HAVE FUN!

Aftercare: sub drop, Top drop, it's not all about the chocolate.

Top Drop, sub drop. These are terms used to describe some of the feelings experienced after a BDSM scene.

You hear a lot about sub drop but not so much about Top drop. I will explore both here as well as what you can do to avoid or alleviate much of the feelings associated with dropping.

What is sub drop? In relative terms sub drop is "coming down" after a scene primarily when a submissive or bottom in the scene reaches subspace. This "coming down" is different with each submissive and should be attended to accordingly. Some people come down slowly and others come down rather quickly. The after affects of coming down can happen within a few minutes to days after a scene.

Drop is something that occurs due to chemical changes in the body during play. Hormones, the release of endorphins, testosterone, and adrenaline, all of these can be wonderful feelings that give us the "high" during play. They also are the primary causes of drop.

It is important for the dominant or top to be aware of this and be prepared to deal with sub drop as the need arises. Sub drop is generally described as feelings of depression or some type of emotion that may display itself in that manner. Sadness, a sense of loss, a feeling of aloneness are some of the feelings that have been described to me when talking about the drop. Of course no two submissives or bottoms are the same and the drop is not the same either. Some people never experience drop and for the most part I believe that this is due to the levels of care given after a scene.

I have seen the gamut of behavior with submissives or bottoms after a scene from giddiness to uncontrolled crying. Sometimes these behaviors will have no rational explanation at all. Sometimes you will have what he/she will describe as the best scene in the world and drop will hit and leave a myriad of feelings that will have you wondering what went wrong. What do you do to deal with this?

The best way to deal with drop is AFTERCARE.

Aftercare is possibly the most important part of a scene next to negotiation. If your play partner is not brand new to the scene, ask during negotiations what he/she usually requires for aftercare. This too can range from being left alone to cuddling and comforting. It is much easier to find out ahead of time then try to wing it during an emotional time.

When doing aftercare, it is important to first take care of any first aid needs there might be after a scene. Most submissives will have a drape or blanket or something of that nature with them to wrap up in after a scene. It is important to make sure that their basic needs are met. They may need something cold to drink. Also have some food items available. Chocolate is also a favorite tool to assist with drop and aftercare.

The submissive might need to sit at your feet for a bit, or be touched, cuddled, held, or may not want to be touched at all. Be sure to allow enough time to make sure that they are taken care of and you will have a play partner that keeps coming back for more.

Some of the other tips you can use:

Be sure to nurture and show care for the bottom.

Talk about your satisfaction with the bottom. Let them know how well they did in the scene and how much you enjoyed it. Thank the bottom for the scene.

Call them a day or two after a scene. Sometimes drop occurs a day or two later. Calling them gives reassurance and confirms your care. Also after a couple of days, feedback can be exchanged to make the scene even better the next time.

Feedback is an important tool for both Top and bottom. Make sure that you include feedback as part of aftercare. This can be done a day or two after the scene or sooner if the submissive is up to it after a scene.

Of course there are exceptions to the whole aftercare rule. If you are playing with someone that has a Dominant, they might prefer to do the aftercare themselves. I have also had scenes where my submissives actually did the aftercare and this was negotiated into the scene. This is usually at a public venue where there are others waiting to use the play station and it is necessary to move your toys out of the way and clean the station for the next scene.

Just as a bottom or submissive experiences drop, so can a top. This also occurs due to the release of chemicals during play. I have been told that I look "stoned" at times after play. I feel stoned after play most of the time due to the chemical releases. This can also lead to that "coming down" feeling and the feelings that go with it.

Some of the things that I have noticed within myself that relate to top drop are usually after very intense scenes or after multiple scenes in one night. I have found that after these events there are times that I experience a depression after a couple of days. These feelings are usually short lived when I recognize them and talk to someone in the lifestyle about the feelings I am experiencing. The emotions are as wide-ranging as those a submissive feels during a drop. I have felt lost, powerless, depressed, melancholy, and even physically sick. Thankfully this is vary rare and not the norm.

I do believe that whether you are Dominant, submissive, Top, bottom, or whatever you call yourself, you should be aware of your feelings as well as your play partner's feelings. Use the important tool of aftercare to avoid a lot of the symptoms of drop or to alleviate them if they do occur. They may never occur, but if they do you will have the information needed to do something about them. Play safe and be healthy and happy in play.

Toys on a Budget: From Pocket Change to Pervertable

I am sure that everyone here has at one time or another drooled over the endless array of toys on the web today. Floggers, cuffs, canes, clamps, whips, and paddles are all abundantly available to us. The problem is that most of us have budgets that we have to follow and with the price of gasoline and other daily necessities, most times we don't have a lot of extra money just lying around to buy a lot of fancy toys. Do we even need fancy toys? NO! Let me give an example.

I travel around the country doing demos for groups and BDSM events. One of the classes that I do is on violet wand play and violet wand fire play. When I first started using a violet wand, I shopped around and found that for a nice kit with all the neat accessories, I would need to spend between 400.00 and 700.00 dollars. Even though the violet wand is still my greatest purchase and most fun toy, which is way too much to spend when there are bills to pay. I got around this price and ended up with a great kit. Here is how:

I bought the wand by itself with a contact probe for 200.00. Then I bought the following accessories:

A bag of Christmas Mylar at a dollar type store. With this I made a nice Mylar flogger. 1.00

A snare drum brush from the music store. 15.00

Metal guitar finger picks for claws. 5 for 2.50

Wartenburg wheel. 8.00

Dental picks. 4.00

Ball Chain 2.00

Glass mushroom attachment. 15.00

Butter knife from home. 0

This comes to a total of 247.50 for the same basic items that are found in a 499.00 kit. The rest of my kit is made up of sharp, pointy metal objects found around the home. I then bought a 7.00 dollar hard plastic handgun case to put the wand and accessories in. It came with foam that I cut to fit all of the items in it. People look at my kit and cannot tell it from any professionally bought expensive kit.

This is an example of the types of things that you can do to cut costs and still have quality toys to play with that are just as evil and fun as the BDSM shop bought items.

One of my favorite places to shop is Dom. Depot (formerly known as Home Depot). You can find a host of items that bring on the best of responses from the bottoms you play with. Some of the items that I have used are rope, yard sticks, clamps in all sizes and tensions, dowel rods, eyebolts, chain, wood for paddles, pulleys, and many more items. The imagination runs wild in a place like that.

I have already mentioned the things that I have bought at the music store. The picks alone make great claws for sensation play. The pet store is a virtual paradise for kinky shopping. Collars, leashes, cages, scalpels, dog toys and accessories for puppy play, and neat metal brushes that work quite well for a variety of sensations.

The local Wal-Mart or other discount store sells some great things for your toy bags. Wooden spoons are great impact toys and leave quite an impression. Vegetable gloves are great for abrasion play. Spatulas, wooden skewers, and basting brushes are a few of the kitchen gadgets that are quite pervertable. You can also find leather strips and scraps, laces, and cloth fabrics in the craft area. If the Wal-Mart has a grocery section, stop off for carrots and cucumbers for insertion play and don't forget the gingerroot for that fine figging adventure.

A trip to the drug store will net you some fine medical play gear. Catheters, enemas, suppositories, bandages, casting supplies, alcohol, condoms to cover toys, lube, gloves, and other items to help with a medical scenario. A small first aid kit is also good to have in your toy bag just in case.

At the local army surplus store, I was able to purchase rope in all colors and diameters for 22 cents a foot. The rope is great for all types of bondage scenes. I also purchased a couple of uniforms from them for some role playing adventures. They also have great boots in stock as well as many knives and other things that can be incorporated into play at great prices if you shop wisely.

The local thrift store is great for costumes for role playing as well as purchasing shoes. I have a good friend that is into cross-dressing and finds great bargains at the thrift store.

The bargains are as great as the imagination when it comes to buying inexpensive items to use for BDSM play. I currently use a suitcase for my rope and bondage gear and a double rifle case for all of my other toys. These were bought at the local sporting goods store at decent prices. If you shop around just a little bit, you will find that you can fill a toy bag in no time with great stuff. I have some pretty expensive floggers, whips, leather restraints, and other things that were purchased from commercial BDSM vendors and stores. They are fun items but I find myself playing with the inexpensive pervertables just as much if not more so with my partners. Try it, you might just surprise yourself with the uses you come up with for every day gadgets.

Switch Dynamics: Who gets tied up tonight?

Dan flips a coin, Michelle calls it in the air…Heads. The coin slowly flips and tumbles its way to the floor. They both wait for it with anticipation. The coin hits the floor and rolls a bit before finally landing in its resting spot. Dan and Michelle peer at the coin, tension mounting. Michelle laughs when she sees the head on the coin. It's going to be a fun night.

I have been around the lifestyle for a number of years. During this time, I have seen a significant change in the way that people view Switches. In BDSM a switch is someone who participates in activities as a top or bottom, a dominant or a submissive.

A good number of people in the lifestyle are either Dominant, or submissive. They either like to give or receive. Switches on the other hand like both sides of that coin. I have heard people in the lifestyle, especially the "old-timers" refer to Switches as "fence riders, greedy, indecisive" etc… That type of idealism seems to be changing with the times. I think that Switches are now becoming more widely accepted, even if still not understood by many.

The fact is, everyone is different, and everyone has their own preferences. I know people who will Top in one scene, and bottom the next in the same night. I also know people that are in Top mode for play, and bottom mode the rest of the time and vice-versa. Some even play games to see who gets to be on top. The combinations are endless. There are a lot of Dominants who swear that they would never submit or bottom to anyone. I think that personally, those that adamantly swear they would never submit or bottom to anyone deep down have an insecurity or ego problem that shows itself in the way that these Dominants take such a defensive stance.

I have heard a number of people that say that they don't have a submissive bone in their body. I have even said that myself. But to some degree, in the world we live in, we submit in one form or another all the time. We have bosses at work, laws of the land, parents, and many other dominant influences in our lives. I hardly think that would classify anyone as Dominant 100% of the time. I do find that when I am in "bottom" mode, I tend to go with the play, but I do not do the "Master, Mistress, Ma'am, or other types of pontificates that people tend to like during play. I just don't have it in me I guess, although it has never been such an issue that kept a scene from happening.

I personally am about 70% Top and 30% bottom. The percentages vary from one person to another. I discovered my switch side after having been a "purist dominant" for almost ten years. It was actually quite by accident. I was speaking to a friend who happened to be a switch. We were talking about various types of sensation play and she asked me if I had ever tried any of this play from the bottom side. Of course for the sake of trying to not sound indignant, I told her that I certainly had not. She laughed and told me that I was truly missing out on all that the lifestyle had to offer by not being willing to open my mind. After lots of challenges from her, that incidentally became negotiations, I did finally bottom to her which opened up a whole new world for me and started a whole new chapter in my journey. From the beginning when she tied me to the bed to the moment that we were cuddling in aftercare, it was truly a rollercoaster ride like none I had ever felt before. I experienced sensations that were unlike any that I had experienced before. The soft feel of rope on my skin. The thudding of a flogger followed by the caress of a soft hand. An intense sting from the canes. The physical portion of this new found way of playing for me was quite exciting and awakening. As far as the mental aspect of the play, I had a wide variety of confused emotions. Fear, pain, guilt, pleasure, excitement, arousal. It took a bit longer to process these feelings and put thing into perspective. All of this created in me a yearning to experience more. I wanted to soar with the rush I felt. I wanted to experience this thing that suddenly seemed to fill a gap in my lifestyle.

I have spoken to numerous switches over time and I think that for me and quite a few others, switching gives us some sense of balance in our lifestyle. I think that it follows the same lines as a successful businessman that is in control of the business on a daily basis. They tend to want to "not be in charge all the time".

The whole reason for switching to me is multifaceted. I like to feel different sensations and experience new things. I like to feel what it is that I am dishing out. I actually have found that I get an endorphin rush from certain types of play that can create a very nice headspace. I get a rush and find that I have a certain "high" from topping that I enjoy. With certain types of play as a bottom, that rush can be much more intense. For instance, I was presenting at an event a couple of years ago. During the play party, I was witness to several piercing scenes. I had seen them before, but for some reason I was intrigued about the sensation. I asked a friend that was well versed in needle play if she would be willing to show me how it feels. Of course this was after talking myself out of trying several times that evening. We were finally set to do this "experiment". I found that from the initial stick of the needle, to the last, the endorphin rush was immediate, intense, and quite lasting. I had never experienced that level as a Top.

I have come to the conclusion that in the big scheme of things, there are no two dynamics in this lifestyle that are the same. I have never seen Master/slave, Top/bottom, or Dominant/submissive relationships that were the same and I have not known any two switches to be the same. There are a number of people out there that are submissive to their Master, but Dominant to everyone else they play with. I know some that are switch couples.

I feel that no matter how we identify, we should be honest with ourselves first, and others second. I feel that we should not hide what we are for the sake of popular opinion. If the whole concept of switches is to become as widely accepted as the other roles people hold in the lifestyle, then we should stand proud in the fact that we get the best of both worlds. For a lifestyle that is supposed to be open to everyone's kinks, sometimes we are quite critical of ourselves and others that don't think exactly the same way. We are not of the same mold and do not have to adhere to others ideas. It's time to break that mold, stand up for what you believe and who you are. Switches of the world UNITE!

Put a Little Spark into Your Play: Violet Wands

Tied to the cross, you cannot see me behind you. The anticipation thick in the air, you shiver as you wait, not knowing what was coming. Suddenly, you hear a buzzing, an unfamiliar electrical sound. The buzzing gets louder as I approach. You jump as I reach and touch your hair, caressing it lovingly before wrapping it in my fist and pulling your head back, laughing that evil little laugh you love to hate. I let go and stand there, letting you hear only the buzzing. Suddenly I touch you with the glowing bulb attached to the end of my Violet Wand. The spark arching from the globe to your skin, the crackling sound fills the room. You jump, startled, trying to process the feeling from the spark. Pain? Pleasure? A mixture of both? The waves of pleasure start to encompass you as I touch you again, running the wand down your thigh…

Erotic electrical play is play like none other. It is edgy. It is great for mind fucking. It is pure pleasure in its rawest form when done correctly. There are a number of different types of electrical instruments out there from a simple Tens Unit to complex Electro Muscle Stimulation (EMS) devices. I would like to focus on the Violet Wand.

I have been using a Violet Wand in play for some time now. It is one of my favorite toys as well as the most popular amongst the bottoms I have played with over time. It is also said by many to be the safest as far as electrical devices that are used in play. It has certainly been a toy that has brought the most intense pleasure to many.

In my experience, it is fairly safe to use the Violet Wand most anywhere on the body except for the head. There are some that disagree with me and say that the head is fine as well. I do not use it above the neck because of the possibility of damage to the eyes if an errant spark made contact with them. If you are first starting out with a Violet Wand and are not quite sure of yourself and its use, you may wish to stay below the chest.

There are a number of ways to play with a Violet Wand. Most of them come with glass attachments of various shapes and sizes. These usually have a gas in them that glow various colors such as violet, hence the name. The attachment is not only a great visual delight with the glow, but also from the sparks that emit from it when you touch yourself or another person. Another attachment is the body contact probe. The probe usually has a cord or chain that has one end that attaches to the wand, and another that you place upon your body or the bottoms, that makes you or them the actual conductor or the electricity. In doing this, you can create a spark on the other person by touching them with your body or metal objects that you hold. The possibilities are endless here. Some of my favorites are dull knifes, tinsel, metal guitar picks, or any number of other articles.

The sensation itself is quite interesting. The sensations can be as mild as a vibration all the way up to a very intense static electricity type shock. The intensity is variable by the control as well as touch. If you directly touch the other person, the feeling might be quite mild. If you start to take your hand away, then the feeling is much more intense. If you hold your hand or the attachments just above the skin, the intensity is a lot greater as the spark jumps the gap.

The violet wand can be quite erotic and cause great sensations or it can be used for intense scenes such as fire play or branding. This is why I highly advocate talking to others that have them in your group or local area. I am sure that others will be willing to show you how to use them safely and correctly. Other options are to attend conventions or demos where violet wand classes are held. There are a number of them around the U. S. and abroad taught by people such as myself that share a love and knowledge of the use and safety of the wand. There are also some things you learn by trial and error. I learned long ago that playing with someone on a bed with a metal rail is fine as long as you do not allow your genital piercing to come into contact with the rail, which really ruined the mood quickly for me I might add.

The Violet Wand can produce some quite pleasurable times for you and your play partner, as long as you follow a few basic rules:

Use of the wand, since it is an electrical device, is inherently a more risky type of play due to the electricity factor.

Some of the attachments out there are shaped in such a way that a person may get the idea to insert them into an available orifice. Do not insert the attachments, as they are glass and can easily break. I don't know many people that take pleasure in explaining to the emergency room personnel why you felt the need to do such a thing. REMEMBER that if you break a toy or play partner, you cannot play with them.

Do not use it around the eyes, on anyone pregnant, with a pacemaker, or other serous ailment. Do not use on people with medical devices such as insulin pumps or medical electronics.

Play safe, use common sense, Play SAFE.

Aftercare, Aftercare, Aftercare. I cannot say that enough. Think about it. We have been taught since we were old enough to stick hairpins in the electrical outlet that electricity is dangerous. If you are playing with someone new to electrical play, it is going to be a scary, mind-fucking, psychologically engaging type of play. Comfort and aftercare are important tools and should be just as much a part of play as negotiations and safety measures.

Although no two scenes are alike for me, typically they have the same basic ingredients when playing with the wand unless I am doing some advanced play such as fire play with the wand. Looking back at a scene not long ago…

After she was undressed, I had her lay on her back on the table. After insuring that she was nicely bound wrists and ankles with my leather restraints, the scene progressed. I picked up the wand, teasing her by running the cool glass globe over her skin. I smile as I turn the wand on, watching her bite her lip in anticipation of what is to come. I show her the wand, its globe flickering a purple hue. The sound coming from it is quite unique. I run the globe over her skin, starting at the shoulders and moving back and forth across her breasts, stopping at her nipples for a moment before moving slowly downward. She gasps as I work my way down her stomach, arching her back and trying to squirm away from the inevitable. I laugh as she squeals and giggles at the sensations of the wand. I increase the intensity of the electricity coming from the wand and move it lower, avoiding her most private areas for the moment. I caress her inner thighs with the magnificent sparks emitting from the wand.

The air is becoming heavy with the ozone that is being produced by the spark. I move the wand up and down her thighs as she starts to quiver, partly from the sharpness of the spark, partly from the pleasure that is building. I move the wand to her mound, just above her clit hood. I lower the wand until the spark makes contact with her hood. She shrieks and tries to pull away from the restraints. I ask her if she is ok. She looks at me and with an almost animalistic growl she begs for more. I place the wand again close to her clit, the sparks dancing across her skin. She is moaning and arching her back as I move the wand in a circular motion around her entire lower body, paying close attention to her clit and cunt. As her moans increase, she spreads her legs more as if willing the sparks to enter into her very core being. She starts to spasm and arches off the table as the first waves of orgasmic bliss start to course through her. I let her ride out this wave and then I turn the wand off and put it down.

I then cover her with her favorite blanket and I hold her as she visits her most special place.

Charge up your play, add a little spark to your night, have fun and play safe...

The art of the MINDFUCK

As I prepare the table for our scene, I ask her once more if she is sure about following through with the scene. She nods at me hesitantly, looking from me to the table. There is a butane torch on the table along with my other toys. I reach into my toy bag and remove a branding iron with my initial on it. I place it next to the torch. I reach into the bag again and take out a blindfold.

She is positioned on bench, restraints securely in place. I walk over and remove the blanket covering her bare ass, lightly swatting her while chuckling at her startled look. I light the torch and place the iron with the tip of it in the flame, watching as my monogram slowly begins to glow. I smile at her again as I brush the hair from her eyes, giving her one last opportunity to bow out of the events that are about to unfold. She nods that she is ready.

I place the blindfold on her. I arrange the table so that everything is within reach. She trembles as I touch her one last time. I tell her to take a deep breath and exhale. I tell her to take another deep breath. As she does so, I press metal to flesh. She screams in agony. I remove the metal from her ass. Her scream changes to a deep sobbing cry. I turn the torch off and lean close to her, speaking softly to her as I embrace her shoulders. As her sobbing begins to subside I take the blindfold and restraints off. I ask her how she feels. She says that it burns. I nod and ask if she wants to see the brand. She nods with a whimper. I take the mirror and hand it to her. She holds the mirror so that she can see the brand site. She looks with disbelief. She lightly touches the brand spot. There is nothing there, not a single mark.

She tells me that she felt the searing pain, heard the torch, saw the flame. I laugh as I hold up the metal pipe that I had removed from the freezer a short time ago. Ice and flame can have the same intensity with the right setup and notions planted.

The mindfuck is an awesome tool. As we know, the mind is the best BDSM tool we have. With the art of the mindfuck, it is easy to plant a notion in the submissive's mind. I can convince my play partner that the toothpick in my hand is a sharp needle that is about to pierce her nipple. I can convince her that the credit card that I am running down her back is the sharp knife I showed her minutes before. If I set the stage right I can convince her that the bottle of water I am pouring down her back is urine or any number of things.

The first time I played with my partner Anita with a knife, I held it to her throat, and also ran it up and down her body, reminding her that it is sharp and can do great damage. Afterwards we talked about the feelings produced by this. She has placed her trust in me and we have played on a number of occasions, but at the instant that the knife blade touched the skin on her neck, things changed briefly. There was the thought that occurred to her that with one slip, one wrong move, or too deep a misplaced trust, and things could become quite dangerous, if not fatal. This, my friends, is the art of the mindfuck.

A well thought out scene coupled with some ingenuity can make for an awesome scene for both the Top and bottom. All that you need to do is practice a bit of theatrics. If you set the stage right then you will be able to alter reality just enough to convince the bottom that an object is something other than what is truly is.

One of the great things about mindfucking is the fact that you don't need fancy crosses, expensive floggers, an awesome dungeon, or any other great tools to make a scene quite rewarding and memorable for both of you. Your only limitations are your imagination.

The mind is susceptible to notions, ideas, and illusion. If we learn to tap into this fun and exciting resource, there is no end to the vast amounts of fun, play, and adventure we can add to our list. One of the key ingredients to a successful D/s relationship of any kind is the ability to "capture the mind". What a great way to start.

I hope that you can use this type of play to enrich and possibly even rekindle that spark that keeps us all cumming back for more.

Into the Abyss: The Fine Art of Vaginal Fisting.

A bottle of water based lube and a pair of gloves. These are the basic tools that you need for a lot of different endeavors. Medical Play, anal play, putting new grips on your golf clubs, and replacing the washers on that leaky faucet are just some of the wonderful uses for these two tools. The one that we are going to discuss today is fisting, specifically vaginal fisting.

The art of vaginal fisting is one that is quite gratifying for the fistee in most cases. There are a lot of women out there that love the feeling of a well-stuffed pussy.

Yes Virginia, a whole hand will fit in your pussy with a little relaxation and time. Even if you're tighter than I am at tax time. For the women that are "size queens" this will be a most fulfilling walk in the park for you, although I don't suggest you try walking anywhere with a cunt full of fist.

As far as fisting goes, there is not a lot of experience involved with vaginal fisting. Anal fisting is a whole other ballgame. It is quite important to take your time, start slow, and work into things so to speak.

So where do we start? It helps to have a comfortable spot with lots of room for the fistee to be able to stretch out and relax. You want the fistee to be as relaxed as possible. I was recently involved in a situation that a friend of mind coined as a "fist-fest". There were several couples in the room with a number of fists in use. This was a truly hot experience. One thing that I think we lacked was plenty of room to stretch out and relax. Be sure that you can do this as it will make things a lot more pleasurable for both of you.

Next to relaxation is arousal. In order for the vagina to open well, the fistee needs to be aroused. If she has a favorite vibrator, tongue, or other type of stimulation that really rocks her world, it would be in your best interest to make use of whatever means necessary to get her juices flowing.

I know that there are a lot of us Domly types out here that love to be in control and do as you please. Fisting is one of those areas where you are a lot better off listening to the fistee and letting them control the speed and depth. This will keep from having to explain to the Dr. later why you have tearing of the vagina.

Now to the juicy stuff:

You should use lots of lubricant and wear gloves. I cannot stress enough that you cannot use too much lube. The lube should be water based. Guys, if you're going to fist your woman, trim your nails. You don't want to damage that delicate tissue that you so love to play with. (Just remember you can't play with your toys if you break them). Coat your entire hand with lube, lots of it. You can also add more as you go.

Start out using a finger or two and take it slow. As she relaxes, you can increase the number of fingers.

You need to make your hand as small as you can. Tuck your thumb and make all of your fingers group so that your hand is as skinny as it can get. I have very large hands and have fisted a number of women successfully the first time they tried.

When you have four fingers in and she is ready for you to proceed, then slowly push in, starting with your knuckles towards her ass. Slowly rotate your hand as you are gently, slowly pushing. The most difficult part of the whole process is getting past the knuckles of your hand. Lube, lube, and more lube. Have the fistee take slow, deep breaths and remind her that she should try to relax. If this is too much for her, then you should stop or back off a bit.

If she is ready to proceed, then you should be able to turn your wrist a little bit to get past the pubic bone. Once you do this, you are in like Flynn. Once inside, the hand will curl up on its own naturally. There are several things you can do once inside.

You should hold still for a moment while you both adjust from the sensation of what has occurred. Then you can move slowly in a rotating motion or move slowly in and out. Do not just start ramming it home once you're inside. Slow and easy till you know what she can handle.

As you are fisting, she might start to contract. If she gets cunt contractions from hell, hang on for all you're worth but do not, DO NOT, pull out suddenly, you can damage muscle and tissue and make it bad for her.

During the Death Grip of the Cunt Monster, it can become quite uncomfortable for you as you feel like a vise is closing around your hand. If she is cumming, then this can feel like you're driving over your hand with a dump truck full of gravel. Trust me, I was not sure that I would have a hand when I pulled out of a couple of fistees.

When she cums……..and she will cum, be prepared for the pussy grip of death, because it will happen. She might even flood the room. I have had fistees that had never squirted before in their life all of a sudden become Niagara falls with a bit of fist play. While she is cumming, let her push you out. This is the best way to disengage from the beast within. If you cannot handle the pain of your hand crushing anymore, let her know so that she can assist you in retrieving your hand from the digit destroyer.

Last but not least. Fisting can be quite an emotional ordeal for the fistee. The trust and closeness that is shared during the fisting is something that should carry over into aftercare. Be aware of your fistee and her feelings, which can run the whole scale from elation to depression and everything in between.

Provide a warm blanket and a quiet, safe, place for her to rest with you close by.

Re-assure the fistee!!! Even if she is unable to take a fist the first, second, or any time at all you should make sure that she is aware that it is ok, and not her fault. Anatomy does not always give you a choice in the matter.

Holding her, talking to her, allowing time to regroup are all ways to assure adequate aftercare. Make sure there is food and drink on hand as well. This should all be a part of most any scene in our lifestyle.

Fisters of the world, UNITE, FIST, and Conquer, One Cunt (and Ass) at a time.

ABUSE VS BDSM

This article is intended to hopefully allow some thought on the differences between abuse and bdsm. As far as I am concerned, this is the most important chapter in the book.

A lot of people in the "vanilla" world tend to associate abuse and bdsm in the same light. Several that I have talked to seem to think that "Tops" or "Dominants" are abusers that use bdsm as a cover for their activities. In a few instances, they are correct. In the years I have been in the lifestyle, I have seen a few rare instances of this happening.

For the most part, People in the BDSM and Leather Communities are genuinely interested in the power exchange and types of play involved. I want to discuss the differences between bdsm and abuse.

What is a Power Exchange vs. Abuse? Here are some Statements to show the difference between the two. Often times people are confused by BDSM and think it is abuse. Here are some ways to tell the difference.

BDSM- Is consensual

Abuse- Is not consensual

What we do with any part of our life having to do with our bodies and the interaction with others is a choice WE make. Regardless of whether you identify as a submissive, slave, bottom, kinky person or whatever the title, your body is your body. You have the final say in what goes on with it.

BDSM- There is an agreed set of rules to play by

Abuse- there are no rules. If there are agreements they are broken and violated

Society has a standard set of rules and laws that people are governed by. As a lifestyle society, we also have standard rules we live by. Some of those include not touching other people's toys or submissives without permission. Another is the fact that just because a person is Dominant, does not mean they are everyone's Dominant.

BDSM- If things get too intense, you are free to use a safe word and it is respected by the top.

Abuse- There are no safe words or they are ignored. Your limits are not respected.

Each of us SHOULD have a safe word in place for play. That safe word should be respected if it is used. For example, I was playing with someone at a party and was using a flogger on them. The flogging got to be too intense for them. At that time they used a safe word that had been prearranged. At that time I stopped what I was doing and talked to them and found that it was too intense and that they needed a break from the flogging for a few minutes. We went on to something else and continued the scene, both enjoying it immensely. When I play,

I use the safe words Yellow and Red. Yellow means to slow down, back off, regroup, and lessen the intensity. Red means STOP. We all have different levels when it comes to sensations and types of play.

BDSM: You are free to be with friends and family in and out of the lifestyle. Your partner encourages you to see your family and friends.

Abuse- You are isolated from your friends and family. Any contact with them is limited if allowed at all.

If the person you are with attempts to cut off your family or friends from seeing you that should be a big warning sign. Another warning sign would be if you were being cut off from your financial resources and things of that nature.

BDSM- You do it because you both enjoy the erotic pleasure you get out of it

Abuse- The abuser does it to feel gratification, and you don't feel good about it.

If we did not enjoy the sensations that were a part of this play, be it spanking, flogging, electrical play, bondage, or any other thing we do for play, then we would not be doing these things. Erotic Power Exchange is just that, an exchange. If you are being abused, you get no enjoyment from whatever the abuser is doing.

BDSM- in BDSM we all have limits that are adhered to.

Abuse- Limits are not respected.

Everyone I know has limits. Some of these limits are SOFT LIMITS, meaning that you do not care to do these things although under a very special circumstance you might consider it. Then there are HARD LIMITS. These are things that you would never do. An example of a hard limit for you might be water sports. If your hard limit is water sports and your partner pees on you in a scene, then the act of not respecting your hard limit is ABUSE.

I know that a lot of us live by the rules of Safe, Sane, and Consensual or by Risk Aware Consensual Kink. Both of these rules have a big thing in common, the word CONSENT. If things are happening between a Top and bottom that are not consensual, then it is abuse.

If you find yourself in this situation, make a plan to get out. Seek help. Call upon others that you are close to. Sometimes intervention by friends is the only way. Don't be afraid to call Law Enforcement if you need to. The important thing is to GET AWAY from the abuser. If you, on the other hand, are an abuser, there is help for you also. You have the power to change this behavior.

I am personally of the opinion that we should live life to its fullest. We should be able to try everything we have ever wanted to experience and we should just plain have fun. Life is too short to do otherwise.

Role-playing: Be All You Can Be -- Or

You lay on the table, your feet in the stirrups. You hear the snap as I put on my gloves, having just completed an overall exam. I place the cold, lubricated speculum at the entrance of your vagina, pushing it gently inside. I open the speculum, spreading you wide, increasing the vulnerable yet somewhat arousing feeling.

Ever wanted to play Doctor? A few dollars for a disposable speculum, gloves, lube, enema bag, a stethoscope. This has all of the makings of a fun night of role-play and fantasy fulfillment.

Role-playing is something that many couples use to enhance their sex lives as well as their relationships as a whole. This is true for vanilla couples as well as couples in the BDSM lifestyle.

I was at a demo a while back that was an interrogation scene. One participant was playing the role of a military interrogator and the other was playing a prisoner of war. The interrogator laid the groundwork by asking the prisoner to simply say a name. It did not have to be a certain name and none was provided, just simply say any name. The scene began with the prisoner tied to a chair. She was nude and there were various torture implements on a table nearby in plain view. The interrogator asked her who the other spy was. She said various things from she didn't know to there are no others. The scene progressed and the "torture" became more intense. Canes, clamps, impact instruments, all came into play. About 45 minutes into this, she finally blurted out a name to ease the torture. It was a very hot, consensual scene.

The scenarios are endless. It does not matter if it is for an enhancement to sex or for the acting out of fantasies in a Power Exchange. We all have fantasies and we each have the ability to act them out in a safe, consensual manner if we chose to. With the popularity of the Internet, we are able to connect with people all over the world to discuss and meet for a variety of reasons, including role-playing.

Role-playing is simply acting out your fantasies in real life. With few exceptions, it does not matter what the fantasy, there is always someone out there that has the reciprocal role of that same fantasy.

The more popular fantasies include:

Nurse/patient

Policeman/criminal

Teacher/student

Interrogator/prisoner

Kidnapper/victim

This is a very short list of role-play roles that can be taken. The list is as great as the imagination. With a little ingenuity, you can be anything you want to be within a role-play scenario. Of course I caution that this, like any other type of play, requires in-depth negotiation as well as complete aftercare, dependent upon the needs of the bottom.

It is of great importance when setting up role-play scenarios that you negotiate completely. There is nothing like getting into the middle of a scene and hitting a trigger that you did not know was there. This can lead to some serious problems as well as stopping what could have been a great, fulfilling scene. Make sure that you know your play partner's limits and anything that should be avoided.

It is also important, especially if you are doing some type of kidnapping scene or something of this nature in a play party setting, to let the Dungeon Monitor or host of the party knows about the scene ahead of time. That way others are aware and do not step into your scene thinking there is something non-consensual occurring.

Role-play has been quite rewarding for a lot of people, myself included. If you have the chance to experience some of these scenes, by all means do so. I think you will find your sex life, as well as play experience, as a whole will become a lot more enriched and fulfilling. Be what you want to be -- and have fun doing it.

Wax Play 101

No, we are not talking Brazilians here.

Wax play is one of the easiest ways to enjoy a nice sensual scene with your partner while adding just the right elements of pain/pleasure and eroticism.

Wax play can be done a number of ways safely and without a lot of expense or physical exertion. One way, and perhaps the most common, is to drip wax from a candle onto your partner. You can also use a paraffin wax with a crock-pot or similar device to melt the wax and use any of a variety of ways to apply it by pouring.

You want to use caution when pouring or dripping the wax so that you do not burn or scald your partner. This tends to make your partner not want to play with you any more in this manner. The best way to regulate the temperature is to hold the candles or wax conveyance at varying distances from your partner. The higher you hold it, the longer the drops have to travel and the more time they have to cool before contact.

One way to add a measure of safety to your play is to test the wax temperature by dripping a few drops on your own wrist or forearm from a variety of heights. This is a good way to make sure that you can come back and play another day.

I would NEVER recommend using beeswax for this type of play. Beeswax burns at a greater temperature than paraffin candles and can cause serious burns. You should also avoid candles with metallic colors as well as scented candles as these burn at higher temperatures also and will burn your partner.

If you use paraffin candles of different colors, you can be quite creative and have great visual stimulation for both you and your partner. Just remember that different colors burn at different temperatures.

If I am going to do a scene with wax, I will take some precautions to assist me with the scene. First off, I will use a drop cloth or old sheet to place under the person that I will be doing the wax play on. This assists me greatly in not having a lot of cleanup afterwards. I am not one that relishes cleaning up large messes after a scene if I do not absolutely have to.

I also have a good sturdy table to put the candles on and I do not leave them lit. I find it safer to light one or two, use them, and then blow them out before putting them down. I don't have to worry about an overzealous partner knocking over a lit candle. It is quite difficult to explain to the fire captain why the house burnt down and why your play partner is covered in wax. I also keep a fire extinguisher handy as well as cold water, ice, wet washcloths and towels. These can come in handy in case of accident.

Be sure to spot test on various areas of the body from various heights. Of course there will be areas of the body that are more sensitive to the heat such as the breasts, pussy, cock, ass, etc. You will want to adjust temperature accordingly. These areas are also the most erotic and can be quite fun to cover in wax. You can use wax just about anywhere and can completely encase body parts such as breasts or a cock.

Do NOT drip hot wax onto someone's face. I also recommend that you don't get wax into hairy parts unless the pain is what you are seeking from hair/wax removal.

After you have played with the wax and are marveling at the great colors, designs, and waxed parts, it is time for removal. A lot of people I know, including myself, remove wax with a knife after the wax has cooled. Using a knife to scrape the wax off is almost as much fun as applying it, both for you and your partner. You can also use vampire gloves or a host of other imaginative ways to remove the wax. After the wax has been removed, you will notice that the skin is quite sensitive. This is an opportune time to try other types of sensation play. You already have ice available. WEG.

Have Fun, Play Safe, and Happy Waxing.

A Short Rambling about me, my humble beginnings, and what drives me.

As I stated before, these articles are for information and education. I do believe that education is the cornerstone of everything we do. A Mentor and dear friend of mine once told me something many years ago that stuck with me to this day. "Always Remain Teachable". What this tells me is that the day I know it all is the day I need to leave the lifestyle I dearly love.

I have found over time that my journey has led me to the Leather Lifestyle. I learn more everyday about that lifestyle, as there are a lot of differences between Leather and BDSM. The Protocol, respect, and honor that come from those sincere about the Leather Lifestyle is what I strive for.

I have been around the BDSM lifestyle since 1992. I have enjoyed many scenes and some not so enjoyable. As far as the Leather Lifestyle, I have been growing in it since around 2002. I first learned of the Leather Lifestyle in the early 1980's and in fact competed in a leather competition in the mid 1980s at a bar called "Our Fantasy" in Wichita, Ks. I had no concept of leather. I was DJing in a gay bar called the R&R. Some friends from the bar took me to a leather bar around the corner from the R. They had a glass showcase with a small assortment of leather items, cock rings, poppers, and lube. They also had a patio that was enclosed and quite private from the outside world. I saw my first flogging, fisting, and male to male sexual contact. My world began changing after that eye-opening night. I still did not grasp enough to jump in until 1992 though.

With the advent of the internet, it has made things so easy for people to meet others of like mind. When I began, I met people through contact magazines that were available in the adult book stores around Wichita. This was practically the only way to meet anyone back then into BDSM or fetish things. I can remember a couple of small BDSM groups that met in peoples homes and only by invite after careful and lengthy screening. These groups never seemed to last for any length of time. The best source for a long time was simply going to the adult bookstore and picking up a "local" swingers type contact magazine and wading through the ads.

I am grateful for the internet and the vast array of information that it has. I am also grateful for the contacts I have made through serving the community on boards, presenting at groups and "conventions", and my writing. I hope that you find something you can use in this book. I will be working on scene specific works in the near future.

Until then, play safe, play smart, and by all means, HAVE FUN!

www.ingramcontent.com/pod-product-compliance
Ingram Content Group UK Ltd.
Pitfield, Milton Keynes, MK11 3LW, UK
UKHW041917190726
13854UKWH00003B/1296

9 781435 724372